SIMPLE to *Sensational* Batiks

Nancy Smith & Lynda Milligan

Book Production

Sharon Holmes – Editor, Technical Illustrator

Susan Johnson – Quilt & Project Designer, Photo Stylist

Lexie Foster – Graphic & Quilt Designer, Photo Stylist

Christine Scott – Editorial Assistant

Sandi Fruehling – Copy Reader

Brad Bartholomew – Photographer

Thanks

Sewers – Jane Dumler, Ann Petersen, Katie Wells, Christine Scott, Lexie Foster

Quilters – Jane Dumler, Ann Petersen

Longarm Quilter – Merrie Martin Jones

Some fabrics provided by Hoffman California Fabrics

Every effort has been made to ensure that the information in this book is accurate. Due to individual skills, conditions, and tools, we cannot be responsible for any losses, injures, or other damages that may result from its use.

POSSIBILITIES®

Fabric Designers for Quilting Treasures™ • Publishers of Possibilities® Books

Home of Great American Quilt Factory, Inc.

www.greatamericanquilt.com • www.possibilitiesquilt.com

1.800.474.2665

Simple to Sensational Batiks

©2008 Nancy Smith & Lynda Milligan

All rights reserved. No part of this book may be reproduced in any form without permission of the authors. The written instructions, photographs, patterns, and designs are intended for the retail purchaser and are protected under federal copyright laws. Projects may not be manufactured for commercial sale. Published by Possibilities® in Denver, Colorado, USA.

ISBN: 1-880972-64-6

From Simple to Sensational

Traditional batik fabrics are dyed with a wax-resist technique, often in a series of repeated steps to add layers of color. Hand-painted and hand-dyed batiks are made without wax and also involve layers and artistic choices as they are created. These fabulous fabrics are truly unique pieces of art. We love using them in our quilts!

Batiks come in a large color range which offers the quilter an almost painterly approach to coloring a quilt. Many shades of a color can be collected which can give a quilt a lovely hand-dyed look. Batiks often have many colors flowing over the yardage, providing a complete palette of color in a single piece of yardage.

There are times, however, that finding just the right color for one of the elements in a "batik quilt" necessitates the use of a fabric other than a batik. Some of our quilts include a marbled or other monochromatic fabric.

We organized **Simple to Sensational Batiks** with quilts ranging from easy to intermediate to challenging. We used the repeating elements throughout, making it possible to start with a simple quilt to learn a technique and then move on to an intermediate quilt, or even directly on to a challenging quilt using the same element or technique.

Of course, you can dive in anywhere based on your own quilting experience and personality! If you want to go directly to one of the challenging quilts, you can always make some practice units or blocks first with scrap fabrics, gaining enough experience to make you feel comfortable with the technique before tackling the whole quilt.

THE ELEMENTS
Straight seams
Applique
Paper piecing
Half-square triangle units
Curved seams

Jump In

Enjoy the simplicity of these first few quilts—they introduce simple straight seams and easy applique.

OCTOBER is a beautiful quilt with very simple cutting and straight seaming. It's perfect for a beginning quilter, for someone who needs a quilt fast, or for someone wanting to learn to choose a collection of over ten batiks that blend into an effective whole.

GUMDROPS takes straight seaming a bit further with Log Cabin piecing. It provides practice in picking monochromatic sets of fabrics to go with a large print.

ROUND AND ROUND is a fun quilt that offers an introduction to simple applique. The scrappy look of this quilt can be accomplished by purchasing fat eighths or using scrap fabrics. Some batiks have enough color variation that cutting from different areas of the yardage yields pieces that appear as if they were cut from separate fabrics.

FALLING LEAVES and LEAF COLLAGE have simple straight seaming of large pieces with the addition of a manageable amount of applique. Be sure to read our applique hint on page 3.

Move On

The addition of half-square triangle units, more extensive paper piecing, and curved seams makes this category intermediate.

VELVET NIGHT utilizes the technique of stitching a small square to a big square to get a floating triangle. We love this technique! When blocks are sewn together, there are no points to match. The addition of a pieced border puts this quilt in the intermediate category.

ARCTIC BLAST is a frigid breath of fresh air— all icy blues and whites. Half-square triangles appear in all parts of this quilt. They can be made from cut triangles, or you can stitch on paper triangles. See our note on page 3 about adjusting yardage when using paper triangles.

From Simple to Sensational _____

SEA FOAM has a wonderful blended look which batiks create so effortlessly. The element in this quilt is half-square triangle units.

TEQUILA SUNRISE is made with the same paper-pieced square that appears in Falling Leaves. Every block can be made exactly the same, like our sample, or the fabrics can be used randomly in the block.

CURVED PLAY introduces curved piecing. The gentle curve is perfect for a first-time experience with the technique. Choosing fabric for this quilt can be a lot of fun, and several choices for purchasing or collecting yardage have been given.

Wow!

The quilts in this category are more challenging. With the experience gleaned from making some of the quilts that appear earlier in the book, they will be very rewarding!

TILTED MOUNTAINS is a quilt that appeared in a national magazine recently. With adaptation to paper piecing, we feel the directions have been simplified, and they fit the scope of this book beautifully. The paper-pieced square is used for the blocks and half the square is used for the green border. The other element in Tilted Mountains is half-square triangle units.

CALYPSO adds the element of more advanced paper piecing in the form of blocks with spiky triangles. Curved seams appear in the paper-pieced block also. Choosing fabrics for this quilt is great fun—wouldn't it also look fabulous in purples and teals?

SOLAR REFLECTIONS rounds out the collection of quilts. It includes more advanced paper piecing plus the elements of applique, curved piecing, and half-square triangles—in other words, it has a little of everything!

We hope you enjoy working your way through our *Simple to Sensational Batiks* quilts!

Odds and Ends

YARDAGE

We love making quilts with lots of fabrics from our stash. Yardage charts for the scrappy quilts have been simplified to give basic yardage with very little waste plus a count of the actual number of fabrics in the quilt so you can choose to purchase the former, the latter, or something in between. Realize that choosing the basic yardage will result in having less fabric left over, but a smaller collection of fabric will make a less scrappy looking quilt. See yardage charts for Round and Round, Velvet Night, and Curved Play.

PAPER TRIANGLES

Paper triangles are great for making half-square triangle units for quilting. They are made by several different companies that use different configurations of squares and diagonal seams, making it difficult to create yardage charts that cover all the possibilities. If you use these patchwork aids for the quilts in this book, please purchase a bit of extra yardage for each of the fabrics involved, just to make sure you have enough.

APPLIQUE HINT

Our books are written for fusible web applique, our method of choice. One great technique is to cut out the fusible web from the back of large shapes to make the applique less stiff. This is very effective when making stacked appliques. Follow manufacturer's directions for tracing shapes to fusible web. Next, cut out the center, leaving a doughnut shape. The margin inside the drawn line can be as little as ¼". Continue by fusing doughnut shaped fusible web to wrong side of fabric. Try this technique for the stacked circles in Round and Round, page 8; the leaves in Falling Leaves, page 10, and Leaf Collage, page 12; and the half-circles in Solar Reflections, page 28.

48 x 60"   6" Block

Yardage Choose fabrics with 42" usable width.

Blocks   ⅜ yd each of 12 fabrics
          browns, tans, greens, golds, rusts, reds
Binding   ⅝ yd
Backing   3¼ yd
Batting   52 x 64"

Cutting Cut strips selvage to selvage.

Blocks   7 pieces 3½ x 6½" of each fabric
          14 squares 3½" of each fabric
Binding   6 strips 2½" wide

Directions

Use ¼" seam allowance unless otherwise noted.

1. BLOCKS: Using fabrics randomly, make 80
   blocks following diagram. Press.

Make 80

2. ASSEMBLE: Arrange blocks as shown in
   diagram. Row 1 has long piece in block at
   top, then at right; then it repeats. Row 2
   repeats right/bottom. Row 3 repeats top/left.
   Row 4 repeats left/bottom. Stitch blocks into
   horizontal rows. Press. Stitch rows together.
   Press.

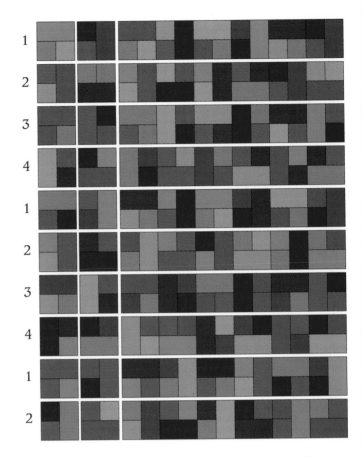

3. LAYER & QUILT: Piece backing horizontally
   to same size as batting. Layer and quilt as
   desired. Trim backing and batting even with
   top.

4. BIND: Stitch binding strips end to end. Press in
   half lengthwise, wrong sides together. Bind
   using ⅜" seam allowance.

Gumdrops

50 x 62"   12" & 6" Blocks

Yardage
Choose fabrics with 42" usable width.

Block centers,
Borders 1 & 3   1½ yd large floral green, yellow, blue, pink
Blocks   ⅜ yd each of 4 greens, 4 yellows,
                4 blues, 4 pinks
Border 2   ⅜ yd
Binding   ⅝ yd
Backing   3⅜ yd
Batting   56 x 68"

Cutting
Cut strips selvage to selvage.

See Steps 1 & 2 for cutting of block centers.

Floral   5 strips 2½" wide - Border 1
            6 strips 4" wide - Border 3
Blocks   start with 1 strip of each fabric 2½"
            wide & 1 strip of each fabric 1½"
            wide - lengths to cut are on diagrams
Border 2   5 strips 2" wide
Binding   6 strips 2½" wide

Directions
Use ¼" seam allowance unless otherwise noted.

1. LARGE BLOCKS: Make blocks as shown using
   4½" square for center and 2½"-wide strips for
   Rounds 1 and 2. Cut centers from any of the
   block fabrics or the large floral. Plenty of fabric
   is allowed. Lengths to cut strips for each round
   are on diagrams. Use all 4 fabrics of each color
   in a round. Press after each round.

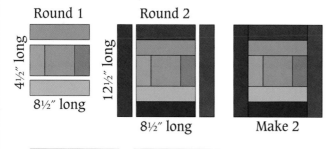

Round 1   Round 2

4½" long   12½" long
8½" long   8½" long   Make 2

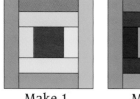

Make 1   Make 1

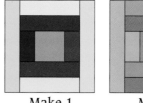

Make 1   Make 1

2. SMALL BLOCKS: Make blocks as shown using
   2½" square for center and 1½"-wide strips for
   Rounds 1 and 2. Cut centers from any of the
   block fabrics or the large floral. Use all 4 fabrics
   of each color in a round. Press after each round.
   Stitch 1 from each set of 6 blocks into a larger
   block of 4 as shown. Make 6. Vary placement
   of small blocks as desired, but keep last strips
   of Round 2 in a vertical position.

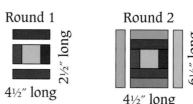

Round 1   Round 2

4½" long   2½" long
            4½" long   6½" long

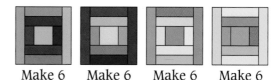

Make 6   Make 6   Make 6   Make 6

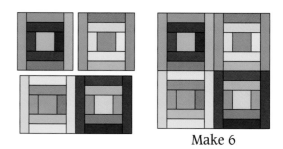

Make 6

3. ASSEMBLE: Arrange blocks as shown in
   diagram on page 31. Stitch into horizontal
   rows. Press. Stitch rows together. Press.

Continued on page 31

42 x 56″   7″ Block

Yardage   Choose fabrics with 42″ usable width.

Blocks
 backgrounds   ⅓ yd each of 10 or more cool colors
           OR 24 fat eighths
           OR 48 scraps 8″ square
           (over 30 fabrics in quilt in photo)
 circles   ⅓ yd each of 10 brights
           OR 24 fat eighths
           OR 144 scraps 3½-7″ square
           (over 60 fabrics in quilt in photo)
Binding   ⅝ yd
Backing   2⅞ yd
Batting   46 x 60″

Cutting   Cut strips selvage to selvage.

Patterns on page 47
Blocks   48 squares 7½″
           48 sets of circles
Binding   6 strips 2½″ wide

Directions

Use ¼″ seam allowance unless otherwise noted.

1. BLOCKS: Using fabrics randomly, applique 48
   blocks with circles centered. See page 3 for
   applique hint. Press.

Make 48

2. ASSEMBLE: Arrange blocks as desired.
   Stitch into horizontal rows. Press. Stitch
   rows together. Press.

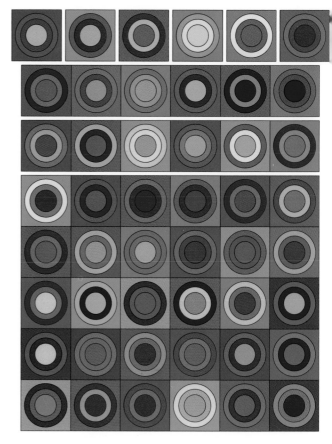

3. LAYER & QUILT: Piece backing horizontally
   to same size as batting. Layer and quilt as
   desired. Trim backing and batting even with
   top.

4. BIND: Stitch binding strips end to end. Press in
   half lengthwise, wrong sides together. Bind
   using ⅜″ seam allowance.

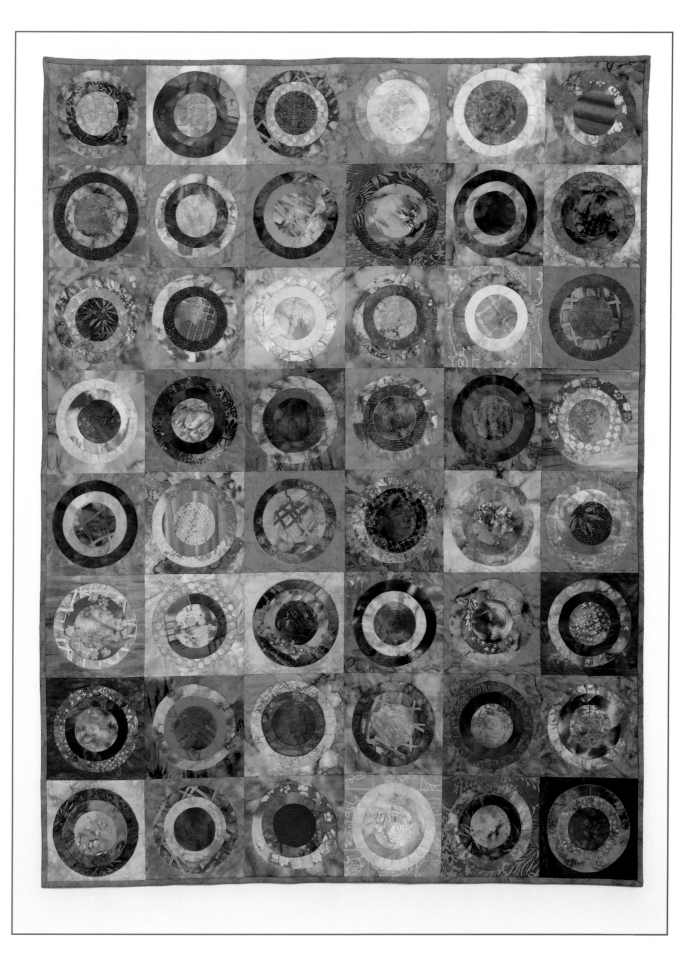

Falling Leaves

42 x 54″

Yardage
Choose fabrics with 42″ usable width.

Dark brown	1⅛ yd
Light brown	⅝ yd
Gold #1	¼ yd
Gold #2	⅓ yd
Dark purple	⅓ yd
Light purple	⅜ yd
Light brown print	⅜ yd
Teal print	⅙ yd
Teal	⅝ yd
Green	½ yd
Binding	⅝ yd
Backing	2⅞ yd
Batting	46 x 58″

Cutting
Cut strips selvage to selvage.

Dark brown	1 piece 19½ x 30½″ - Piece 1
	2 pieces 5½ x 26½″ - Border 2
	2 pieces 5½ x 10½″ - Border 2
Light brown	1 piece 6½ x 24½″ - Piece 2
	2 strips 5½″ wide - Bdr 2 right
Gold #1	1 piece 4¼ x 11¾″ - Piece 6
Gold #2	1 piece 8 x 11¾″ - Piece 7
Dark purple	1 piece 8 x 18½″ - Piece 8
Light purple	1 piece 4¼ x 14¾″ - Piece 4
	1 leaf #2 - pg 41
Light brown print	1 piece 4¾ x 24½″ - Piece 3
	1 piece 2⅛ x 41¾″ - Bdr 1 left
	1 piece 2⅛ x 32½″ - Bdr 1 top
Teal print	1 piece 1⅝ x 41¾″ - Bdr 1 right
	1 piece 1⅝ x 32½″ - Bdr 1 bottom
Teal	2 strips 5½″ wide - Bdr 2 left
	1 square 4¼″ - Piece 5
	1 leaf #1 - pg 41
Green	1 leaf #3 - pg 41
Binding	6 strips 2½″ wide

Directions
Use ¼″ seam allowance unless otherwise noted.

1. PAPER-PIECED BLOCKS: After cutting pieces 1-8, Borders 1 and 2, and leaves, cut 2½ x 7½″ pieces as needed from remaining fabric. For center panel, paper piece 2 blocks as shown using fabrics randomly. For Border 2, paper piece 2 blocks as shown using fabrics randomly in center and border fabric on ends. Pattern on page 39. Trim 3 blocks to sizes shown. Press.

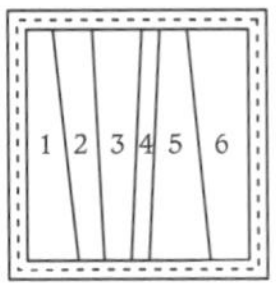

Cut paper ¼″ outside dotted line

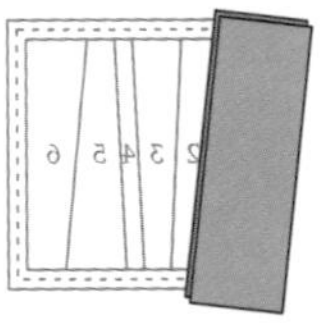

Place first 2 strips right sides together - place on back of paper pattern, edges ¼″ beyond line between 1 & 2

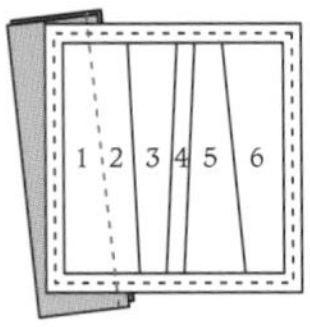

Turn over & stitch on line between 1 & 2

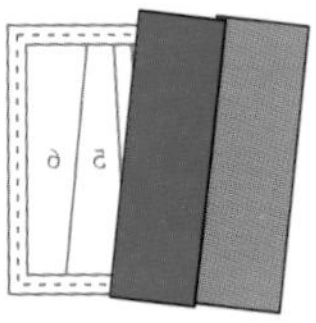

Turn over & press strip 2 to right side

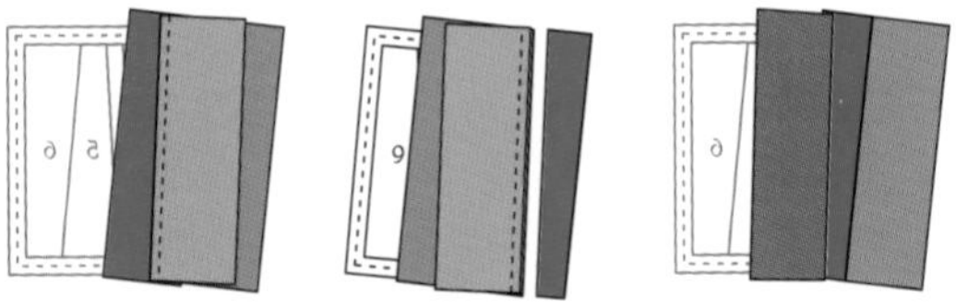

For Center Panel

Make 2   Trim 1 to 4¾″ wide

Repeat with remaining strips: Place edge of each new strip ¼″ (or more) beyond seam line - stitch - fold back paper & trim strips, leaving ¼″ seam allowance - press new strip to right side

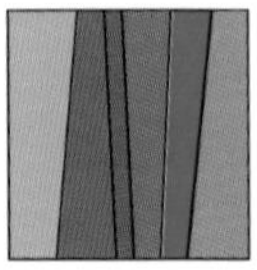

Trim block on dotted line - remove paper now or after block is sewn into quilt

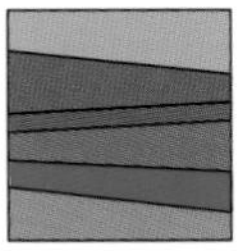

For Border 2

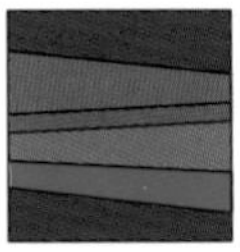

Make 2 with border fabric on ends   Trim both to 5½″ wide

Continued on page 30

Leaf Collage

44x44″

We suggest that you label the fabrics.

Yardage
Choose fabrics with 42″ usable width.

Cream	¼ yd
Light tan	⅝ yd
Dark tan	⅞ yd
Light brown	⅔ yd
Med/dark brown	⅔ yd
Dark gray-brown	⅛ yd
Dark brown	⅙ yd
Purple/pink	½ yd
Greens	⅙ yd each of 2 fabrics
	⅛ yd each of 2-4 fabrics
Binding	½ yd
Backing	3 yd
Batting	48x48″

Cutting
Cut strips selvage to selvage.

Cream	1 square 2½″ - Unit 1
	1 piece 2½x9½″ - Unit 2
	1 piece 4½x5½″ - Piece 3
Light tan	6 squares 2½″ - Unit 1
	2 pieces 2½x22½″ - Unit 1
	1 piece 4½x5½″ - Piece 4
	1 piece 10½x34½″ - Piece 12
Dark tan	1 square 2½″ - Unit 1
	2 pieces 3½x4½″ - Unit 3
	2 pieces 3½x10½″ - Unit 3
	1 piece 8½x8½″ - Piece 2
	1 piece 2½x22½″ - Piece 6
	2 strips 4½″ wide- Piece 14
Light brown	1 square 2½″ - Unit 1
	1 piece 2½x4½″ - Unit 2
	1 piece 10½x24½″ - Piece 10
	1 piece 6½x34½″ - Piece 11
Med/dark brown	1 square 2½″ - Unit 1
	2 squares 2½″ - Unit 2
	1 piece 10½x24½″ - Piece 9
	1 piece 6½x10½″ - Piece 13
Dark gray-brown	1 piece 1½x22½″ - Piece 7
Dark brown	1 square 2½″ - Unit 1
	1 piece 1½x15½″ - Piece 5
	1 piece 2½x24½″ - Piece 8
Purple/pink	2 pieces 2½x2½″ - Unit 2
	1 piece 4½x4½″ - Unit 3
	1 piece 13½x13½″ - Piece 1

Greens	see Step 5 - patterns on page 42
Binding	5 strips 2½″ wide

Directions
Use ¼″ seam allowance unless otherwise noted.

1. UNIT 1: Using pieces labeled Unit 1 in cutting chart, make 1 following diagram. Press.

Unit 1 - Make 1

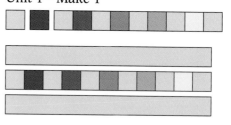

2. UNIT 2: Using pieces labeled Unit 2 in cutting chart, make 1 following diagram. Press.

Unit 2 - Make 1

3. UNIT 3: Using pieces labeled Unit 3 in cutting chart, make 1 following diagram. Press.

Unit 3 - Make 1

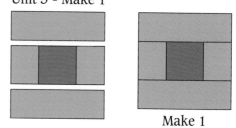

Make 1

4. ASSEMBLE: Stitch strips for Piece 14 end to end. Press. Cut 1 piece 44½″ long. Using pieces labeled 1-13, new piece 14, and Units 1-3, assemble top following diagrams. Press each seam after it is sewn.

Continued on page 35

Velvet Night

55 x 64" 9" Block

Yardage
Choose fabrics with 42" usable width.

Blocks	⅓ yd each of 15 or more fabrics (27 in quilt in photo) blacks, golds, purples, plums, fuchsias
Border 1	⅞ yd black
	⅙ yd each of 2 purples
Border 2	⅝ yd purple
Binding	⅝ yd
Backing	3¾ yd
Batting	61 x 70"

Cutting
Cut strips selvage to selvage.

Blocks	for each block:
	8 squares 3½" - background
	1 square 3½" - center
	8 squares 2" - star points
Border 1	3 strips 2" wide - black
	3 strips 3½" wide - black
	4 squares 3½" - black
	30 pieces 2 x 3½" - black
	30 squares 2" of each purple
Border 2	6 strips 2½" wide
Binding	7 strips 2½" wide

Directions
Use ¼" seam allowance unless otherwise noted.

1. BLOCKS: Using 3 fabrics in each block, make 30 blocks following diagrams. Press.

For each block, make 4 side units

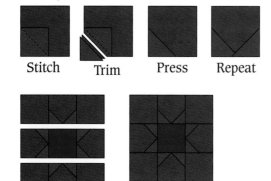

Stitch   Trim   Press   Repeat

Make 30

2. ASSEMBLE: Arrange blocks as desired. Stitch into horizontal rows. Press. Stitch rows together. Press.

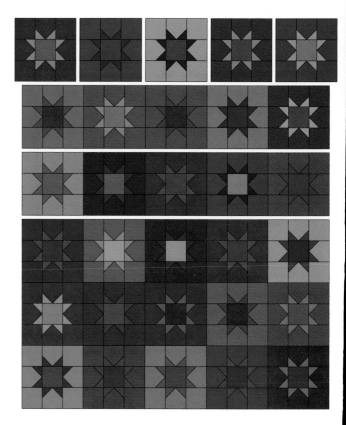

3. BORDER 1: Make 30 units as shown below. Stitch into 2 borders of 15 each. See diagrams on bottom of page 31. These should measure 45½" long or be the same width as quilt center. Adjust seams if necessary. Set aside.

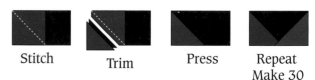

Stitch   Trim   Press   Repeat
Make 30

Stitch 2"-wide strips end to end. Press. Cut 2 pieces 45½" long or the same width as quilt center. Set aside.

Stitch 3½"-wide strips end to end. Press. Cut 2 pieces to fit sides of quilt. Stitch to sides of quilt. Press. See diagram on page 31.

Assemble parts for top and bottom border units as shown in diagrams on bottom of page 31. This includes 3½" squares for ends. Press. Stitch top and bottom borders to quilt. Press.

Continued on page 31

14

Arctic Blast

64 x 64″   2″, 4″, & 8″ Units

See diagram at right for parts of quilt.

We suggest that you label the fabrics.

Yardage   Choose fabrics with 42″ usable width.

Backgrounds	⅞ yd each of 3 fabrics
	1 white, 2 very light blues
Light blues	⅞ yd light greenish blue #1
	⅓ yd light greenish blue #2
	⅝ yd light blue
Med blues	¼ yd med greenish blue #1
	½ yd med greenish blue #2
	½ yd each of 2 med blues
Dark blues	⅝ yd each of 2 fabrics
Binding	⅝ yd
Backing	4⅛ yd
Batting	70 x 70″

Cutting   Cut strips selvage to selvage.
*Cut in half diagonally.

Backgrounds

white	1 square 8½″ - center
	*8 squares 2⅞″ - center
	8 squares 6½″ - large star
	8 squares 4½″ - Border 2
very lt blue #1	*2 squares 4⅞″ - center
	4 pieces 2½ x 8½″ - center
	8 pieces 4½ x 12½″ - Border 1
very lt blue #2	*8 squares 4⅞″ - large star
	*4 squares 8⅞″ - large star
	*8 squares 4⅞″ - Border 1

Light blues

lt greenish #1	*4 squares 6⅞″ - large star
	*6 squares 8⅞″ - Border 2
lt greenish #2	*4 squares 6⅞″ - large star
light blue	*6 squares 8⅞″ - Border 2

Medium blues

med greenish #1	*8 squares 2⅞″ - center
med greenish #2	*2 squares 4⅞″ - center
	8 squares 4½″ - Border 2
med blue #1	*8 squares 4⅞″ - large star
	*8 squares 4⅞″ - Border 1
med blue #2	*4 squares 8⅞″ - large star
	4 squares 4½″ - Border 1
Dark blues	*6 squares 8⅞″ of each - Bdr 2
Binding	7 strips 2½″ wide

Directions

Use ¼″ seam allowance unless otherwise noted.

1. CENTER: Use pieces labeled center in cutting chart to make one following diagrams. Press.

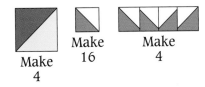

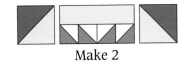

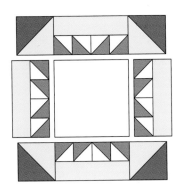

Continued on page 32

56 x 77″   12″ Block, 3″ Sashing Unit

We suggest that you label the fabrics.

Yardage

Choose fabrics with 42″ usable width.
Purchase extra fabric if seaming Border 3 diagonally.

Blocks
- ½ yd blue/green/purple check
- ⅓ yd blue #1 - blue block center triangles
- ⅜ yd blue #2 - blue block star points
- ⅜ yd blue #3 - blue block side unit bkground
- ⅓ yd blue #4 - blue block corners
- ½ yd green #1 - green block center triangles
- ¾ yd green #2 - green block star points
- ¾ yd green #3 - green block side unit bkgrnd
- ½ yd green #4 - green block corners

Sashing
- ⅙ yd each of 8 or more blues & greens
- ⅙ yd each of 8 or more creams
- ⅜ yd blue/green/purple check - corners

Border 1   ⅝ yd
Border 2   ⅜ yd
Border 3   1 yd
Binding   ⅝ yd
Backing   3¾ yd
Batting   62 x 83″

Cutting

Cut strips selvage to selvage.
*Cut in half diagonally.
**Cut in quarters diagonally.

Blue blocks
- 4 squares 6½″ - check
- 16 squares 3½″ - blue #1
- 32 squares 3½″ - blue #2
- 16 pieces 3½ x 6½″ - blue #3
- 16 squares 3½″ - blue #4

Green blocks
Square
- 3 squares 6½″ - check
- 12 squares 3½″ - green #1
- 24 squares 3½″ - green #2
- 12 pieces 3½ x 6½″ - green #3
- 12 squares 3½″ - green #4

Triangular
- **3 squares 9¾″ - green #1
- 40 squares 3½″ - green #2
- 20 pieces 3½ x 6½″- green #3
- 10 squares 3½″ - green #4
- **5 squares 5½″ - green #4

Sashing
- *48 squares 3⅞″ - blues & greens
- *48 squares 3⅞″ - creams
- 8 squares 3½″ - check - inside squares
- **2 squares 5½″ - check - side triangles
- *2 squares 3″ - check - corner triangles

Border 1   6 strips 2½″ wide
Border 2   6 strips 1½″ wide
Border 3   7 strips 4½″ wide
Binding   7 strips 2½″ wide

Directions

Use ¼″ seam allowance unless otherwise noted.

1. BLUE BLOCKS: Make 4 blue blocks. Press.

For each blue block:

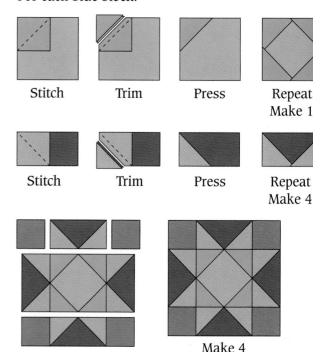

Stitch   Trim   Press   Repeat Make 1

Stitch   Trim   Press   Repeat Make 4

Make 4

2. GREEN BLOCKS: Make 3 green blocks for center of quilt (square) and 10 green blocks for sides of quilt (triangular). More diagrams on page 38. Press.

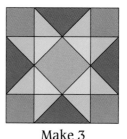

Make 3

Continued on page 38

18

Tequila Sunrise

46 x 58″ 6″ Block

Yardage

Choose fabrics with 42″ usable width.

Paper-pieced blocks	½ yd each of 6 brights
Plain blocks,	
Four-patch blocks	⅜ yd each of 4-5 brights
	⅓ yd dark
Border 1	⅓ yd
Border 2	⅞ yd
Binding	⅝ yd
Backing	3¼ yd
Batting	52 x 64″

Cutting

Cut strips selvage to selvage.

Paper-pieced blocks	5 strips 2½″ wide from each paper-piecing fabric
Plain blocks	18 squares 6½″
Four-patch blocks	12 squares 3½″
	12 squares 3½″ dark
Border 1	5 strips 1½″ wide
Border 2	6 strips 4½″ wide
Binding	6 strips 2½″ wide

Directions

Use ¼″ seam allowance unless otherwise noted.

1. PAPER-PIECED BLOCKS: Cut strips for paper piecing into 7½″ segments. Paper piece 24 blocks referring to diagrams on page 10. Pattern on page 39. Press.

Make 24

2. FOUR-PATCH BLOCKS: Make six blocks as shown, with dark in opposite corners and brights in opposite corners. Press.

Make 6

3. ASSEMBLE: Arrange blocks as shown. Stitch into horizontal rows. Press seam allowances toward plain blocks and four-patch blocks. Stitch rows together. Press.

4. BORDER 1: Stitch strips end to end. Press. Cut 2 side borders to fit quilt. Stitch to sides of quilt. Press. Repeat at top and bottom.

5. BORDER 2: Repeat Step 4.

6. LAYER & QUILT: Piece backing horizontally to same size as batting. Layer and quilt as desired. Trim backing and batting even with top.

7. BIND: Stitch binding strips end to end. Press in half lengthwise, wrong sides together. Bind using ⅜″ seam allowance.

21

Curved Play

35 x 35″   7″ Block

Yardage
Choose fabrics with 42″ usable width.

Blocks ⅓ yd each of 25 or more fabrics
blues, greens, purples, pinks
OR 25 or more fat eighths
OR 50 scraps at least 9x9″
(40 fabrics in quilt in photo)

Binding ⅛ yd each of 5-7 fabrics (not needed if
purchasing ⅓-yd pieces or fat eighths)

Backing 1¼ yd

Batting 39 x 39″

Cutting
Cut strips selvage to selvage.

Patterns on page 40

Blocks 25 from Pattern A, 25 from Pattern B

Binding 1 strip 2½″ wide of each fabric (or
pieces 2½″ wide by varying lengths -
see Step 4)

Directions

Use ¼″ seam allowance unless otherwise noted.

1. BLOCKS: Using fabrics as desired, pin and
   stitch blocks together as shown with background piece on top. Press seam allowance
   toward background.

Match
centers

Pin
center

Pin
ends

Make 25

2. ASSEMBLE: Arrange blocks as shown or make
   your own arrangement. Stitch into horizontal
   rows. Stitch rows together. Press.

3. LAYER & QUILT: Cut backing to same size
   as batting. Layer and quilt as desired. Trim
   backing and batting even with top.

4. BIND: Cut pieces of binding of varying
   lengths, from 6″ to 30″ long. Stitch pieces
   end to end to a finished length of 160″. Press
   in half lengthwise, wrong sides together. Bind
   using ⅜″ seam allowance.

Made and owned by Ann L. Petersen—a class sample for curved piecing

Tilted Mountains

65 x 83"   9" Block

Directions for this quilt have been simplified with paper piecing since its appearance in a national magazine, so quilt in photo varies slightly from quilt in diagrams and directions.

Yardage
Choose fabrics with 42" usable width.
Purchase extra fabric if seaming Border 3 diagonally.

Blocks   ½ yd ea of 9 purples - paper-pieced squares
          ⅙ yd ea of 20 purples & greens -
          triangles & small squares
Border 1 ⅜ yd red-purple
Border 2 ⅜ yd each of 7 bright greens
Border 3 1½ yd purple
Binding   ⅔ yd
Backing   5¼ yd
Batting   71 x 89"

Cutting
Cut strips selvage to selvage.
*Cut in half diagonally.

Blocks   5 strips 2½" wide from each
          paper-piecing fabric
          *140 squares 3⅞" - cut in sets of 2
          35 squares 3½"
Border 1 6 strips 1½" wide
Border 2 4 strips 2½" wide from each fabric
Border 3 7 strips 6½" wide
Binding   8 strips 2½" wide

Directions
Use ¼" seam allowance unless otherwise noted.

1. BLOCKS: Cut strips for paper piecing into 7½" segments. Using fabrics randomly, paper piece 35 blocks referring to diagrams on page 10. Pattern on page 39. Press. Make 140 half-square triangle units in sets of 4. Press. Group block elements for 35 blocks—1 paper-pieced square, 1 set of 4 triangle units, and one 3½" square. Make 18 blocks with large squares oriented as shown. Repeat for 17 blocks with large squares turned 90°. Press.

For each block:

Make 1

Make 4

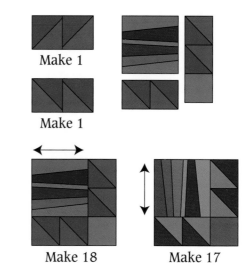
Make 1

Make 1

Make 18   Make 17

2. ASSEMBLE: Arrange blocks, alternated as shown. Stitch into horizontal rows. Stitch rows together. Press.

3. BORDER 1: Stitch strips end to end. Press. Cut 2 side borders to fit quilt. Stitch to sides of quilt. Press. Repeat at top and bottom.

Continued on page 37

Calypso

59 x 71″   6″ Block

Yardage   Choose fabrics with 42″ usable width.

Blocks &
Border 2	⅓ yd each of 30 brights OR 30 fat quarters
Border 1	½ yd green
Border 2	1⅜ yd dark red
Border 3	¾ yd orange-red
Border 4	⅜ yd dark red
Border 5	⅝ yd orange-red
Binding	⅝ yd
Backing	3⅞ yd
Batting	65 x 77″

Cutting   Cut strips selvage to selvage.

Patterns on pages 43-44

If trying to match quilt exactly, make 12 sets of 2 blocks with same pieced arc and Piece C fabrics, but with Piece A cut from different fabrics.

Plain blocks	4 squares 6½″
4-patch blocks	56 squares 3½″
Plain-arc blocks	6 sets A, B, & C (see Step 2)
Pieced-arc blocks	24 A, 24 C
	72 pieces 2½ x 4½″ - rays
	96 pieces 3½ x 4½″ - background
Border 1	5 strips 2½″ wide
Border 2	from 1⅜-yd red piece:
	13 strips 2½″ wide
	5 strips 1″ wide
	from fabrics left from blocks:
	92 pieces 2½ x 4½″
	4 squares 4″ - corners
Border 3	6 strips 3½″ wide
Border 4	6 strips 1½″ wide
Border 5	7 strips 2½″ wide
Binding	7 strips 2½″ wide

Directions

Use ¼″ seam allowance unless otherwise noted.

1. FOUR-PATCH BLOCKS: Make 14 four-patch blocks, using fabrics randomly. Press.

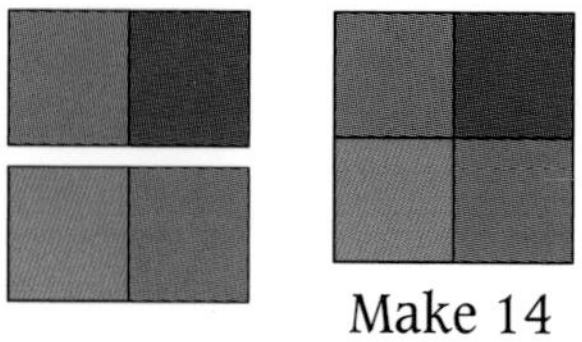

Make 14

2. PLAIN-ARC BLOCKS: Ignoring wedge lines and numbers on Pattern B, page 43, make 6 plain-arc blocks. Use fabrics randomly. Press. See page 22 for curved piecing diagrams.

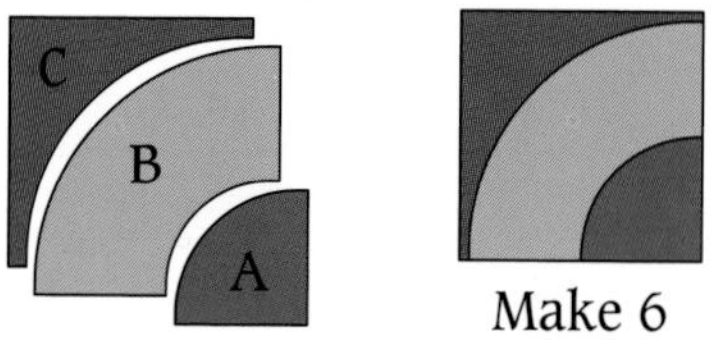

Make 6

3. PIECED-ARC BLOCKS: Using Pattern B, page 43, and referring to diagrams for paper-pieced square on page 10, make 24 paper-pieced arcs. Assemble 24 blocks with Pieces A, C, and paper-pieced arcs (B). Press.

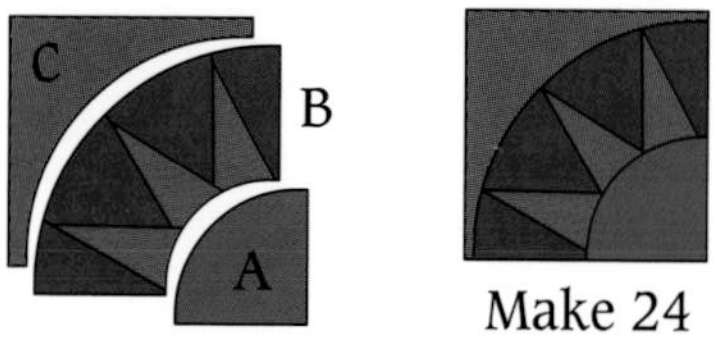

Make 24

4. ASSEMBLE: Stitch blocks into 4-block units as shown. Press. Stitch into horizontal rows. Stitch rows together. Press.

26

Continued on page 36

Solar Reflections

50 x 50" 8" Block

We suggest that you label the fabrics.

Yardage
Choose fabrics with 42" usable width.

Blocks
- ⅓ yd blue - Blocks A & B Piece E
- ½ yd lt purple - Block D Piece E, Block C medium half-circle
- 1 yd yellow - Block A Piece B, Blocks C & E Piece E
- ½ yd tan - Blocks A & B ray background
- 1⅜ yd gold - Blocks D & E ray background
- ⅓ yd each yellow, orange, gold, rust, brown - Blocks A, D, E rays
- ⅓ yd brown #1 - Block B rays, Block A Piece A
- ⅓ yd rust - Blocks B, D, & E Piece A, Block C large half-circle
- ⅙ yd dark tan - Block B Piece B
- ⅓ yd orange - Block B Piece C, Blocks C & E Piece B
- ⅓ yd brown #2 - Blocks A, D, & E Piece C
- ⅛ yd dark purple - Block C small half-circle, Flying Geese border corners

Flying Geese
Border
patchwork:
- ⅙ yd each brown, rust, orange
- ⅙ yd each of 4 blues
- ⅙ yd yellow - plain strips
- ¼ yd rust - plain strips

Border 1	⅓ yd
Border 2	¾ yd
Binding	⅝ yd
Backing	3¼ yd
Batting	54 x 54"

Cutting
Cut strips selvage to selvage.

Patterns on pages 45-47

Blocks A, B
- 2 A brown #1, 2 A rust
- 2 B yellow, 2 B dark tan
- 2 C brown #2, 2 C orange
- 4 E blue
- 4 strips 3½" wide - tan
- 2 strips 2½" wide - brown #1
- 1 strip 2½" wide of each ray fabric

Blocks D, E
- 12 A - rust
- 12 B - orange
- 12 C - brown #2
- 4 E - lt purple
- 8 E - yellow
- 11 strips 3½" wide - gold
- 2 strips 2½" wide of each ray fabric

Block C
- 4 squares 8½" - yellow
- 4 large half-circles - rust
- 4 medium half-circles - lt purple
- 4 small half-circles - dk purple

Flying Geese
Border
- 24 pieces 1½ x 2½" of each brown, rust, orange
- 36 squares 1½" of each blue
- 2 strips 1½" wide - yellow
- 4 strips 1½" wide - rust
- 4 squares 2½" - dk purple

Border 1	5 strips 1½" wide
Border 2	5 strips 4½" wide
Binding	6 strips 2½" wide

Continued on page 33

Block A

Block B

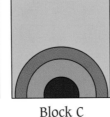

Block C

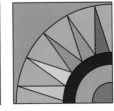

Block D

Block E

28

Falling Leaves
Continued from page 10

2. CENTER PANEL: Stitch 6½″ paper pieced block to end of Piece 2. Press. Stitch this unit to Piece 1. Press. Stitch 4¾″ paper pieced block to end of Piece 3. Press. Stitch this unit to Piece 1. Press. Stitch Pieces 4-6 together as shown. Press. Stitch to center panel. Press. Stitch Pieces 7 and 8 together as shown. Press. Stitch to center panel. Press.

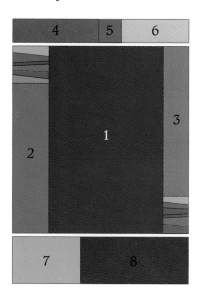

3. BORDER 1: Stitch side border pieces to quilt. Press. Stitch top and bottom border pieces to quilt. Press.

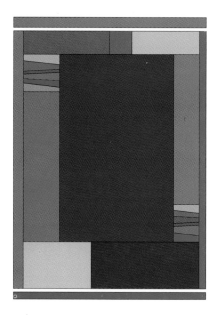

4. BORDER 2: Stitch teal strips end to end. Press. Cut a piece 44½″ long. Repeat with light brown strips. Stitch side border pieces to quilt. Press. Stitch paper-pieced block between one long and one short brown border piece. Press. Repeat. Stitch one to top and one to bottom of quilt as shown. Press.

5. APPLIQUE: Applique leaves to quilt using photo as a guide for placement. See page 3 for applique hint.

6. LAYER & QUILT: Piece backing horizontally to same size as batting. Layer and quilt as desired. Trim backing and batting even with top.

7. BIND: Stitch binding strips end to end. Press in half lengthwise, wrong sides together. Bind using ⅜″ seam allowance.

Gumdrops
Continued from page 6

Velvet Night
Continued from page 14

4. BORDER 1: Stitch strips end to end. Press. Cut 2 side borders to fit quilt. Stitch to sides of quilt. Press. Repeat at top and bottom.

5. BORDERS 2 & 3: Repeat Step 4.

6. LAYER & QUILT: Piece backing horizontally to same size as batting. Layer and quilt as desired. Trim backing and batting even with top.

7. BIND: Stitch binding strips end to end. Press in half lengthwise, wrong sides together. Bind using ⅜″ seam allowance.

4. BORDER 2: Stitch strips end to end. Press. Cut 2 pieces to fit sides of quilt. Stitch to sides of quilt. Press. Repeat at top and bottom.

5. LAYER & QUILT: Piece backing horizontally to same size as batting. Layer and quilt as desired. Trim backing and batting even with top.

6. BIND: Stitch binding strips end to end. Press in half lengthwise, wrong sides together. Bind using ⅜″ seam allowance.

Velvet Night Border 1

Make 2

Make 2

Arctic Blast
Continued from page 16

2. LARGE STAR: Use pieces labeled large star in cutting chart to make large star units and stitch them to center. Press.

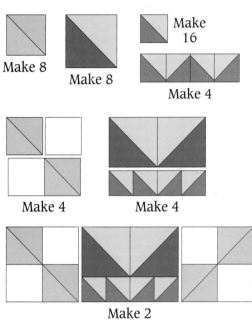

Make 8

Make 8

Make 16

Make 4

Make 4

Make 4

Make 2

3. BORDER 1: Use pieces labeled Border 1 in cutting chart to make border units and stitch them to quilt top. Press.

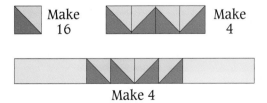

Make 16

Make 4

Make 4

4. BORDER 2: Use pieces labeled Border 2 in cutting chart to make border units and stitch them to quilt top. Press.

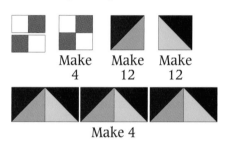

Make 4

Make 12

Make 12

Make 4

5. LAYER & QUILT: Piece backing to same size as batting. Layer and quilt as desired. Trim backing and batting even with top.

6. BIND: Stitch binding strips end to end. Press in half lengthwise, wrong sides together. Bind using ⅜″ seam allowance.

Solar Reflections

Continued from page 28

Directions

Use ¼" seam allowance unless otherwise noted.

1. CENTER BLOCKS: Cut all paper-piecing strips into 5½" segments. Using pattern piece D on page 45, and referring to diagrams for paper-pieced square on page 10, make 4 ray units colored as shown below. Assemble 4 blocks with Pieces A, B, C, E, and paper-pieced ray units (D). Press. Stitch 4 blocks together as shown. See page 22 for curved piecing diagrams.

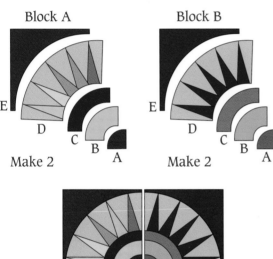

Block A   Block B

E   D   C   B   A

Make 2   Make 2

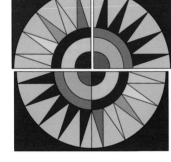

2. FLYING GEESE BORDER:

Cut 2 pieces from yellow strips 16½" long. Stitch to sides of center unit. Cut 2 pieces 18½" long and stitch to top and bottom Press.

Make 72 Flying Geese units as shown using same blue fabric on both sides of each unit. Press. Stitch into 4 borders of 18 units each. Press. Stitch 2 to sides of center unit, oriented as shown. Press. Stitch dark purple corner squares to each end of remaining units. Press. Stitch to top and bottom of center unit, oriented as shown. Press.

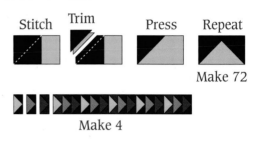

Stitch   Trim   Press   Repeat

Make 72

Make 4

From rust strips, cut 2 pieces 22½" long. Stitch to sides of center unit. Cut 2 pieces 24½" long and stitch to top and bottom. Press.

3.

OUTER BLOCKS:

Applique 4 side blocks with half-circles. Match raw edges of background square and half-circles. See page 34 for diagrams and page 3 for applique hint.

Continued on page 34

33

Solar Reflections

Continued from page 33

Block C Block D Block E

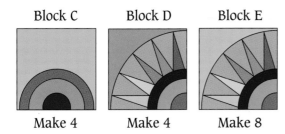

Make 4 Make 4 Make 8

Make 4

Make 4 ray blocks with light purple corners and 8 with yellow corners, as shown at left. (This is a simplification from the quilt in the photo in which half of each of the types of ray blocks are made mirror image.)

Use diagrams as guides for orientation. Make 4 border units with blocks C and E. Stitch 2 to sides of quilt. Stitch a block D to each end of each remaining unit. Press. Stitch to top and bottom. Press.

4. BORDER 1: Cut 2 strips to fit sides of quilt. Stitch to sides of quilt. Press. Stitch remaining strips end to end. Press. Cut 2 pieces to fit top and bottom of quilt. Stitch to top and bottom of quilt. Press.

5. BORDER 2: Stitch strips end to end. Press. Cut 2 to fit sides of quilt. Stitch to sides of quilt. Press. Repeat at top and bottom.

6. LAYER & QUILT: Piece backing to same size as batting. Layer and quilt as desired. Trim backing and batting even with top.

7. BIND: Stitch binding strips end to end. Press in half lengthwise, wrong sides together. Bind using ⅜″ seam allowance.

Leaf Collage

Continued from page 12

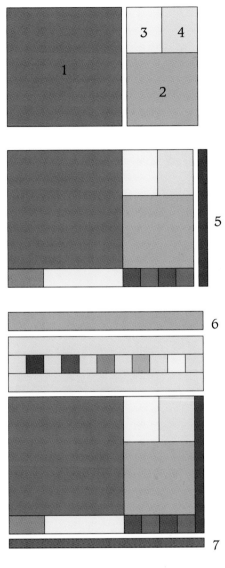

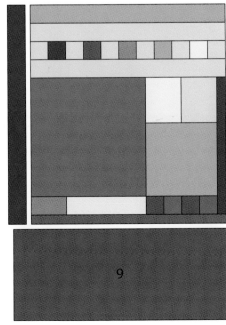

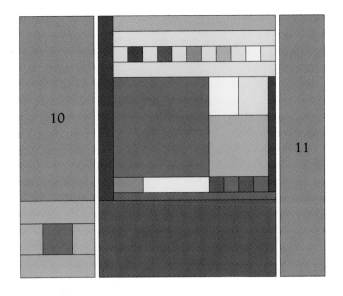

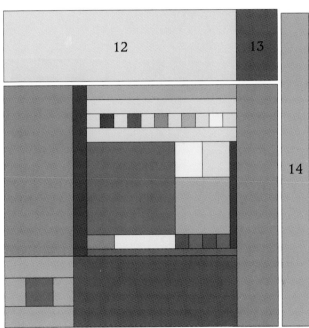

5. APPLIQUE: Follow directions on page 42 for sizing patterns and tracing. Use ⅙-yd pieces for large leaf. Use remaining fabrics as desired. Applique leaves to quilt using photo as a guide for placement. See page 3 for applique hint.

6. LAYER & QUILT: Piece backing to same size as batting. Layer and quilt as desired. Trim backing and batting even with top.

7. BIND: Stitch binding strips end to end. Press in half lengthwise, wrong sides together. Bind using ⅜″ seam allowance.

Calypso

Continued from page 26

5. BORDER 1: Stitch strips end to end. Press. Cut 2 pieces to fit sides of quilt. Stitch to sides of quilt. Press. Repeat at top and bottom.

6. BORDER 2: Cut 2½″ red strips for paper piecing into 4½″ segments. Using these segments and pieces cut from block fabrics, make a total of 20 units from the Center Section pattern, 2 units from the shaded area of the Center Section pattern, 4 units from the Right End pattern, and 4 units from the Left End pattern. Patterns on page 44. Refer to diagrams for paper-pieced square on page 10. Assemble units as shown below. Press.

Stitch 1″-wide strips end to end. Cut 2 pieces to fit side border patchwork units. Stitch to side patchwork units. Press. Repeat with top and bottom patchwork units. Stitch squares to ends. Press. Stitch side borders to quilt. Press. Repeat with top and bottom borders.

7. BORDERS 3, 4, 5: Repeat Step 5.

8. LAYER & QUILT: Piece backing horizontally to same size as batting. Layer and quilt as desired. Trim backing and batting even with top.

9. BIND: Stitch binding strips end to end. Press in half lengthwise, wrong sides together. Bind using ⅜″ seam allowance.

For each side border:

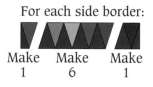

Make 1   Make 6   Make 1

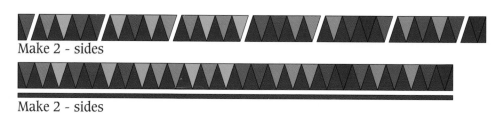

Make 2 - sides

Make 2 - sides

For each top/bottom border:

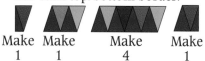

Make 1   Make 1   Make 4   Make 1

Make 2 - top & bottom

Make 2 - top & bottom

Tilted Mountains

Continued from page 24

4. BORDER 2: Cut strips for paper piecing into 4½″ segments. Using fabrics randomly, make 40 units from shaded portion of paper-piecing pattern. Press. Stitch into borders as shown, trimming ends as needed to fit quilt. Stitch side borders to quilt. Press. Stitch top and bottom borders to quilt. Press.

5. BORDER 3: Repeat Step 3.

6. LAYER & QUILT: Piece backing vertically to same size as batting. Layer and quilt as desired. Trim backing and batting even with top.

7. BIND: Stitch binding strips end to end. Press in half lengthwise, wrong sides together. Bind using ⅜″ seam allowance.

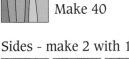 Make 40

Sides - make 2 with 11 sections each   Trim

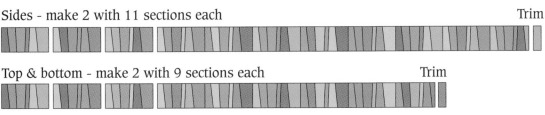

Top & bottom - make 2 with 9 sections each   Trim

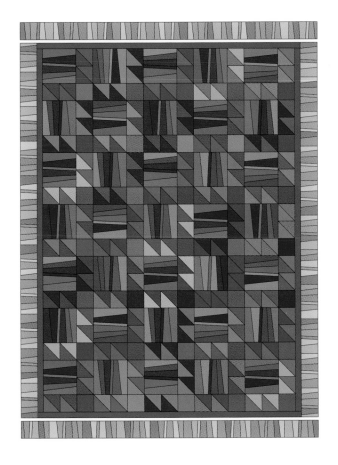

Sea Foam
Continued from page 18

For each side block:

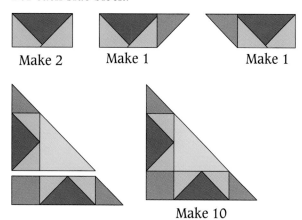

Make 2   Make 1   Make 1

Make 10

3. SASHING: Make 96 half-square triangle units with creams on one side, blues and greens on other side. Press. Stitch into 24 units of 4, half facing one way and half the other. Press.

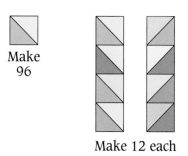

Make 96

Make 12 each

4. ASSEMBLE: Arrange blocks, sashing units, side triangles, and corner triangles as shown at top right. Second diagram clarifies vertical placement of seams and direction of dark side of each unit. Stitch into diagonal rows. Stitch rows together. Press.

5. BORDERS 1, 2, & 3: Stitch strips end to end. Press. Cut 2 side borders to fit quilt. Stitch to sides of quilt. Press. Repeat at top and bottom.

6. LAYER & QUILT: Piece backing horizontally to same size as batting. Layer and quilt as desired. Trim backing and batting even with top.

7. BIND: Stitch binding strips end to end. Press in half lengthwise, wrong sides together. Bind using ⅜" seam allowance.

Tilted Mountains

Make 75 copies. Use 6½″ square pattern for blocks and grayed pattern for border.

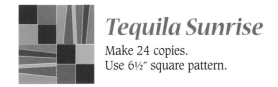

Tequila Sunrise

Make 24 copies.
Use 6½″ square pattern.

Falling Leaves

Make 4 copies. Use 6½″ square pattern.

Use grayed part
of pattern for
border of
Tilted Mountains

| 1 | 2 | 3 | 4 | 5 | 6 |

| 1 | 2 | 3 | 4 | 5 | 6 |

Use 6½″ square
pattern for blocks of
Tilted Mountains,
Tequila Sunrise,
& Falling Leaves

For clarity in small diagrams on page 10, grayed
portion of this pattern is deleted.

Permission granted to copy for personal use

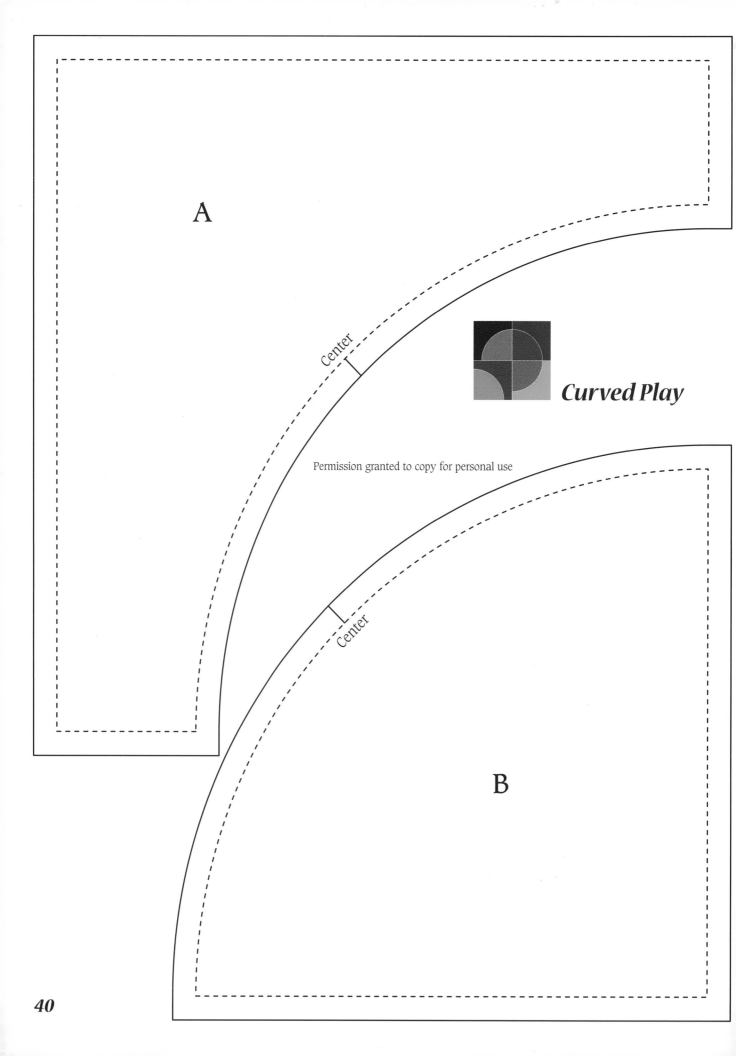

A

Center

Curved Play

Permission granted to copy for personal use

Center

B

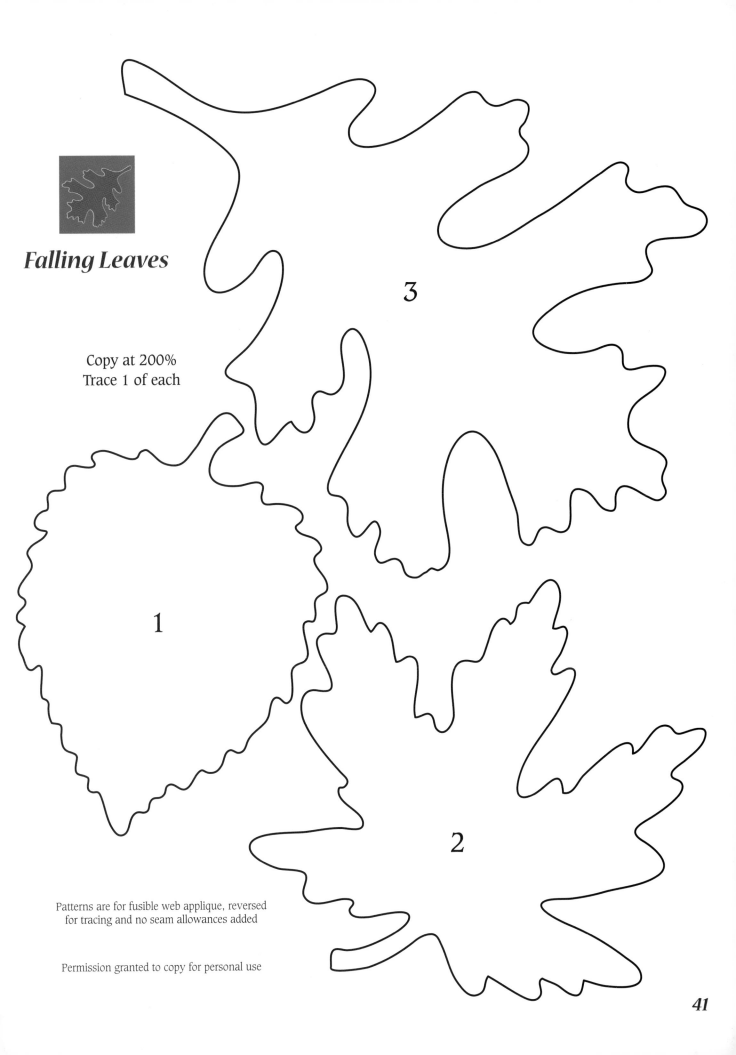

Falling Leaves

Copy at 200%
Trace 1 of each

3

1

2

Patterns are for fusible web applique, reversed
for tracing and no seam allowances added

Permission granted to copy for personal use

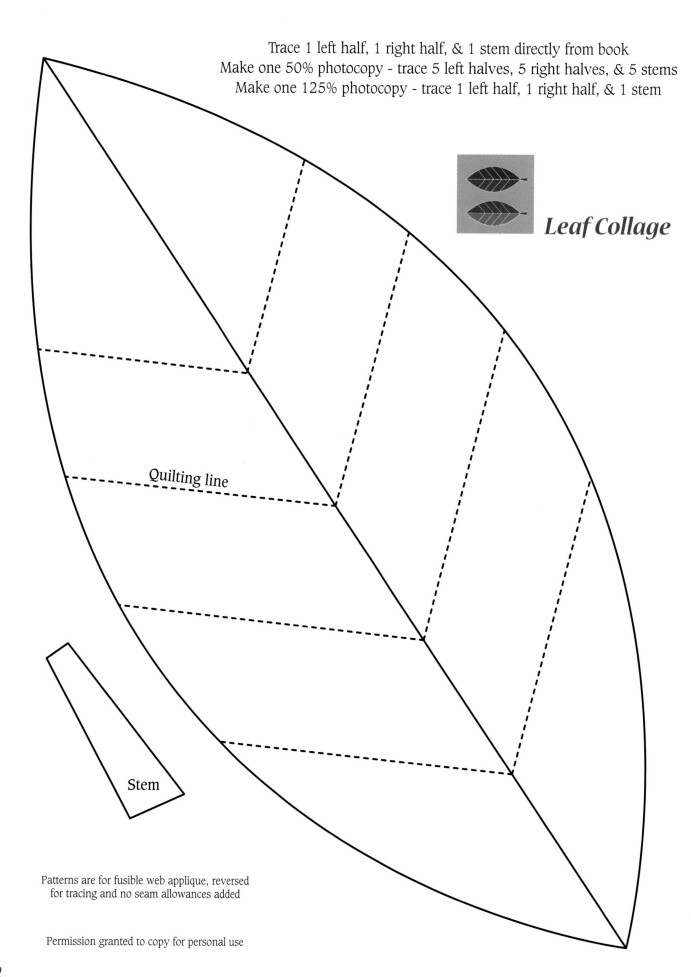

Trace 1 left half, 1 right half, & 1 stem directly from book
Make one 50% photocopy - trace 5 left halves, 5 right halves, & 5 stems
Make one 125% photocopy - trace 1 left half, 1 right half, & 1 stem

Leaf Collage

Quilting line

Stem

Patterns are for fusible web applique, reversed
for tracing and no seam allowances added

Permission granted to copy for personal use

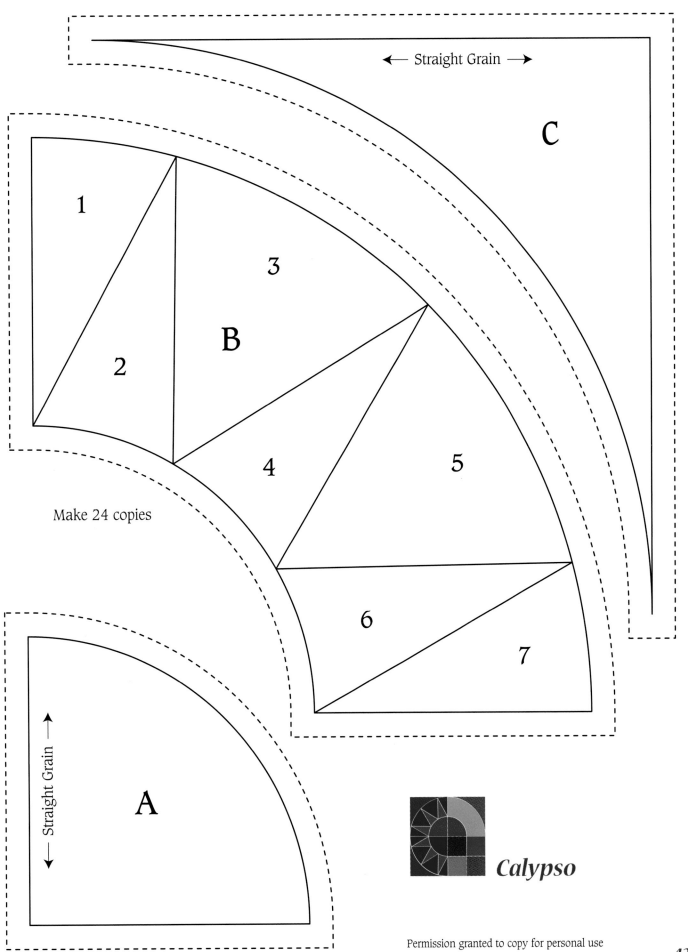

← Straight Grain →

C

1

3

B

2

4

5

Make 24 copies

6

7

Straight Grain →
←

A

Calypso

Permission granted to copy for personal use

Calypso

Left End Section

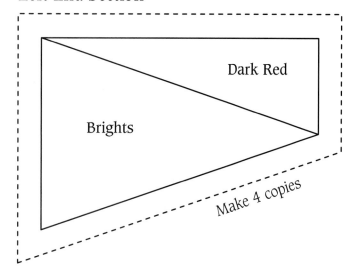

Dark Red

Brights

Make 4 copies

Right End Section

Make 4 copies

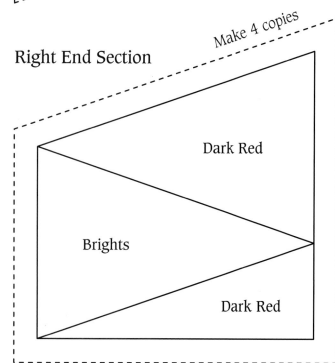

Dark Red

Brights

Dark Red

Center Section

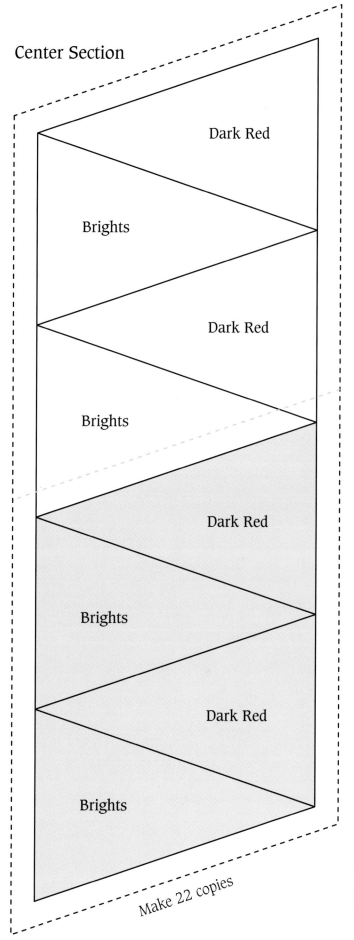

Dark Red

Brights

Dark Red

Brights

Dark Red

Brights

Dark Red

Brights

Make 22 copies

Permission granted to copy for personal use

44

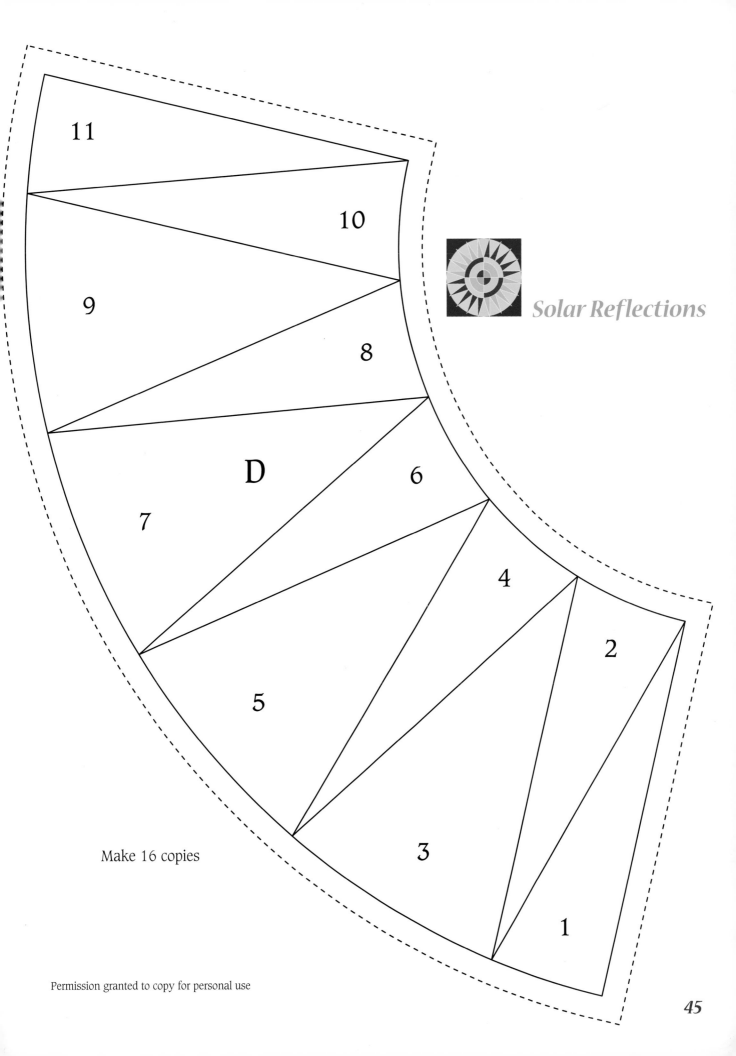

11

10

9

8

D

6

7

4

2

5

3

1

Make 16 copies

Solar Reflections

Permission granted to copy for personal use

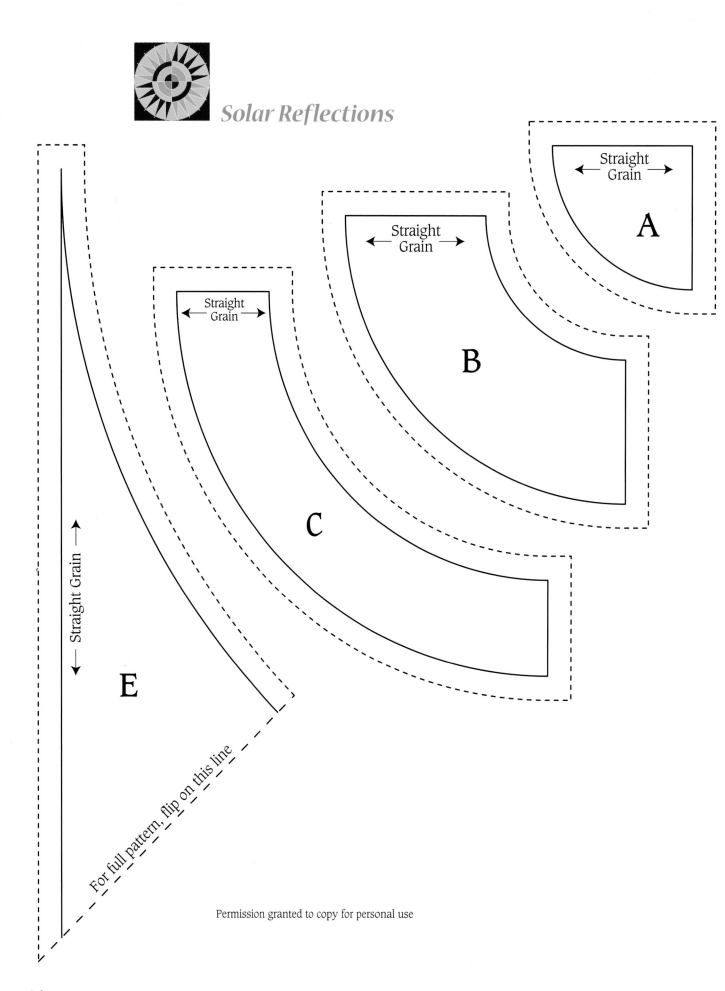

Solar Reflections

Straight Grain

A

Straight Grain

B

Straight Grain

C

Straight Grain

E

For full pattern, flip on this line

Permission granted to copy for personal use

Solar Reflections

Lines 1, 2, 4 - half circles
including seam allowance

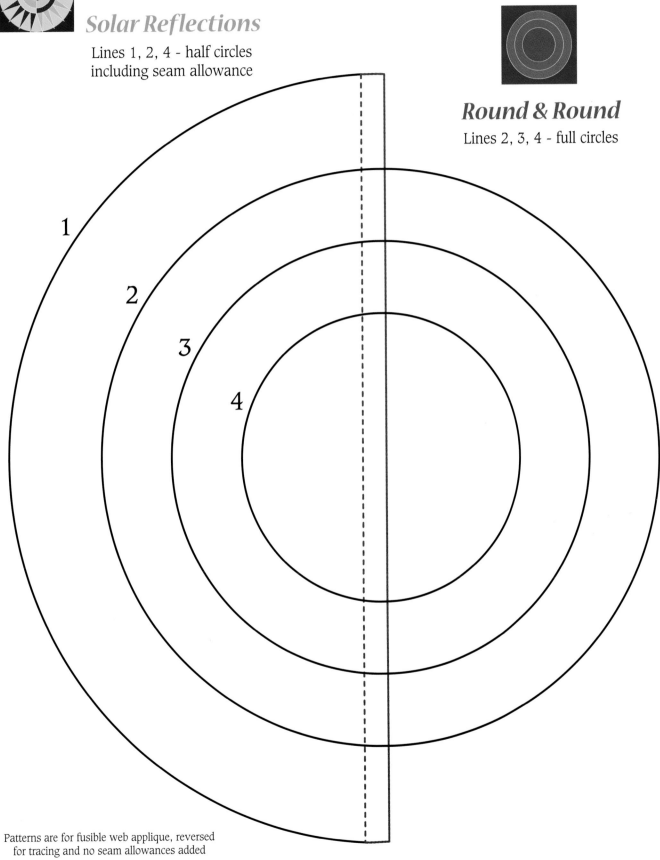

1

2

3

4

Round & Round

Lines 2, 3, 4 - full circles

Patterns are for fusible web applique, reversed
for tracing and no seam allowances added

Permission granted to copy for personal use

20 quilts and
wall hangings that
celebrate friendship
$26.95

Favorite quilt patterns
that can be made in five
different sizes
$19.95

21 charming quilts for
babies, toddlers, and
young children
$22.95

18 super simple quilts
using packets of 6½"
squares or strips
$18.95

Cabin in the Woods
quilt with 13 other
projects that use
elements taken from
the main pattern
$19.95

15 different quilts to
display on beds,
couches, or tables
$21.95

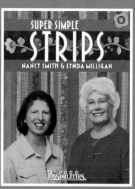

18 fantastic quilts to
create from precut 6½"
strips or yardage
$18.95

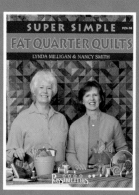

Patterns for 12 quilts
using all those
fat quarters you've
been collecting
$18.95

3 cute seasonal quilts
plus 6 other smaller
quilts made from the
same elements
$19.95

13 dynamic pineapple
quilt patterns for all
skill levels
$21.95

16 unique quilt
patterns using various
triangle methods
$19.95

13 delightful quilt
patterns and 21 unique
small projects to make
for children
$21.95

Choose creative projects
from three main themes:
*Gingerbread, Santa
Claus, & Poinsettia*
$22.95

Wildflower Sampler quilt
with 16 other projects
that use elements taken
from the main pattern
$22.95

This pattern lends
itself to many different
fabric combinations
$9.95

POSSIBILITIES®

Phone 303-740-6206 • Fax 303-220-7424 •
Orders only U.S. and Canada 1-800-474-2665 • www.possibilitiesquilt.com

9017708077

CHRIS PACKHAM

AMAZING ANIMAL
JOURNEYS

ILLUSTRATED BY JASON COCKCROFT

RED
SHED

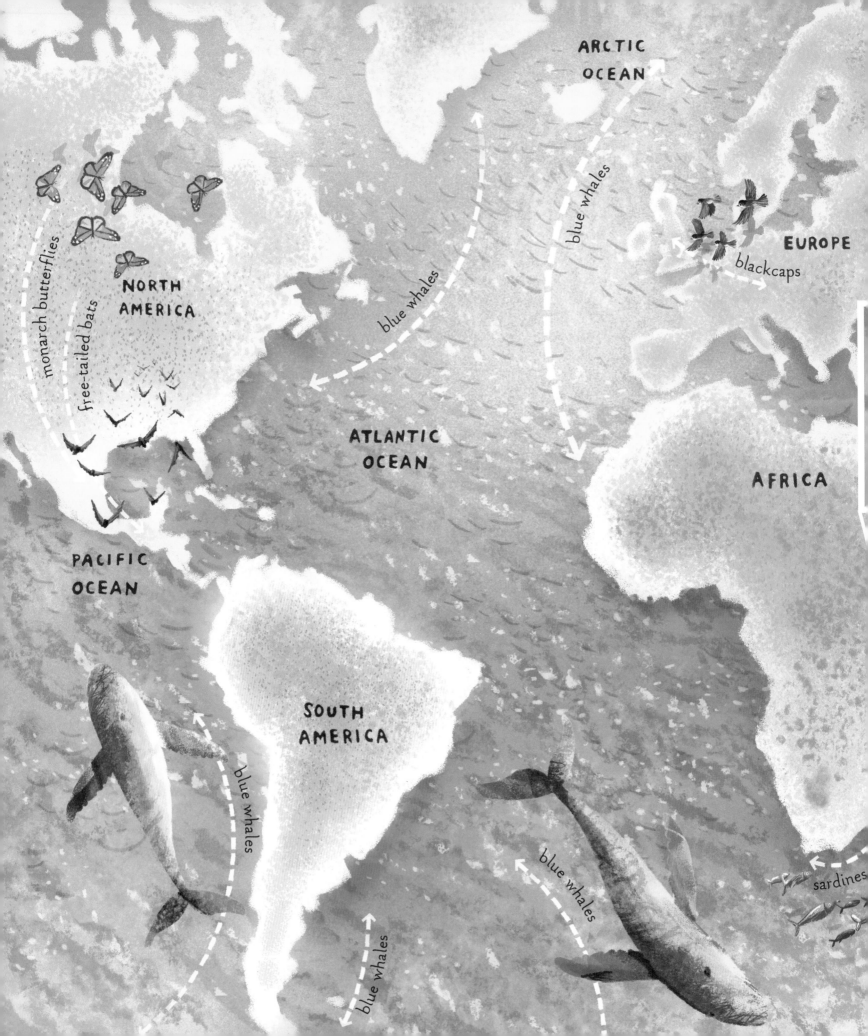